How to Write Effective Requirements for IT
Simply Put!

Use Four Simple Rules to Improve the
Quality of Your IT Requirements

Thomas Hathaway
Angela Hathaway

Copyright © 2016 BA-EXPERTS

Ordering Information:

Quantity sales. Special discounts are available on quantity purchases by corporations, associations, and others. For details, contact the publisher at books@BusinessAnalysisExperts.com.

The content of this book is also available as an eCourse at http://businessanalysisexperts.com/product/video-course-writing-requirements/

ISBN-10: 1519261594
ISBN-13: 978-1519261595

DEDICATION

This work is dedicated to future generations of Business Analysts, Product Owners, Subject Matter Experts, Domain Experts, COOs, CEOs, Line Managers, and anyone responsible for representing the business community's interests on an Information Technology project.

CONTENTS

DEDICATION i

CONTENTS ii

ACKNOWLEDGMENTS iv

PREFACE v

Setting the Stage for Writing Effective Requirements 9

    Why Do You Need Better Requirements? 9

    Managing Uncertainty 13

    THE Question File 19

    Exercise: The Subjectivity of Language 22

    The "Real" Problem with Requirements............................23

Capturing Requirements 27

    Follow the KISS concept..28

    A Complete Sentence Forces a Complete Thought 32

    Exercise: Simple, Complete, and Well-Structured....................36

    Define the Business Need 37

    Exercise: Avoiding the Elusive "How" 41

Requirements and Project Scope.............................. 43

    Keep Your Requirements in Scope...............................44

    Exercise: Relevant Requirement Components 47

    Combat Scope Creep from the Start............................48

Exercise: Testing the Scope Boundaries 54

Recap of Rules One through Three.. 55

Exercise: Applying the First Three Rules................................... 56

Finding and Fixing Ambiguous Requirements 59

Who Needs to Understand Your Requirements?..................... 60

Roadblocks to Effective Requirements.................................... 62

Desk-Checking Uncovers Ambiguity 65

Exercise: Finding Ambiguity with the SME 66

Use Peer Reviews to Increase Understandability..................... 67

Exercise: Requirement Interpretations 72

Combatting the Major Cause of Project Failure 73

Exercise: Revising Requirements to Reduce Ambiguity 78

Best Practices for Improving Understandability.....................81

Use Acronyms and Corporate Standards 82

Exercise: Using Revisions to Reduce Ambiguity 85

Add Context to Eliminate Ambiguity 86

Exercise: Appropriate Context Reduces Ambiguity.................. 90

Write to the Readability Level of Your Audience 91

Exercise: Using Readability Indices... 94

Recap Rule Four 95

Exercise: Rule Four Applied 96

Where Does Your Path Go from Here? 99

ABOUT THE AUTHORS 100

ACKNOWLEDGMENTS

This publication would not have been possible without the active support and hard work of our daughter, Penelope Hathaway. We would also be remiss if we did not acknowledge the thousands of students with whom we have had the honor of working over the years. We can honestly say that every single one of you influenced us in no small way.

Finally, we would like to acknowledge Harvey, the fictional Pooka created by Mary Chase and made famous by the movie of the same name with James Stewart. Very early in our marriage we recognized that a third entity is created and lives whenever we work closely on a concept, a new idea, or a new product. Over the years, this entity became so powerful and important to us that we decided to name it Harvey and he should rightfully be listed as the author of this and all of our creative works. Unfortunately, Harvey remains an invisible being, living somewhere beyond our physical senses but real nonetheless. Without Harvey, neither this book nor any of our other publications would have been possible. For us, Harvey embodies the entity that any collaborative effort creates and he is at least as real as each of us. We would truly be lost without him.

PREFACE

Writing requirements is one of the core competencies for anyone in an organization responsible for defining future Information Technology (IT) applications. However, nearly every independently executed, root-cause analysis of IT project problems and failures in the past half-century have identified "misunderstood or incomplete requirements" as the primary cause. This has made writing requirements the bane of many projects. The real problem is the subtle differences between "understanding" someone else's requirement and "sharing a common understanding" with the author.

"How to Write Effective Requirements for IT – *Simply Put!*" gives you a set of 4 simple rules that will make your requirement statements more easily understood by all target audiences. The focus is to increase the "common understanding" between the author of a requirement and the solution providers (e.g., in-house or outsourced IT designers, developers, analysts, and vendors).

The rules we present in this book will reduce the failure rate of projects suffering from poor requirements. Regardless of your job title or role, if you are tasked with communicating your future needs to others, this book will help. It includes optional exercises with instant feedback to increase retention.

Who should read this book?

Anyone involved in capturing, writing, analyzing, or understanding requirements for Information Technology solutions, including (but not limited to):

- ✓ Subject Matter Experts (SME)
- ✓ Agile Product Owners
- ✓ Business Process Managers
- ✓ Business Process Users

✓ Business Analysts
✓ and anyone wearing the BA hat

Regardless of your title or role, if you are involved in defining requirements, this book is for you. Specifically, this book will give you techniques to:

⇨ Express business and stakeholder requirements in simple, complete sentences

⇨ Write requirements that focus on the business need

⇨ Test the relevance of each requirement to ensure that it is in scope for your project

⇨ Translate business needs and wants into requirements as the primary tool for defining a future solution and setting the stage for testing

⇨ Create and maintain a question file to reduce the impact of incorrect assumptions

⇨ Minimize the risk of scope creep caused by missed requirements

⇨ Ensure that your requirements can be easily understood by all target audiences

⇨ Confirm that each audience shares a common understanding of the requirements

⇨ Isolate and address ambiguous words and phrases in requirements.

⇨ Use our Peer Perception technique to find words and phrases that can lead to misunderstandings.

⇨ Reduce the ambiguity of a statement by adding context and using standard terms and phrases

How to get the most out of this book?

To maximize the learning effect, you will have optional, online exercises to assess your understanding of each presented technique. Chapter titles prefaced with the phrase "Exercise" contain a link to a web-based exercise that we have prepared to give you an opportunity to try the presented technique yourself.

These exercises are optional and they do not "test" your knowledge in the conventional sense. Their purpose is to demonstrate the use of the technique more real-life than our explanations can supply. You need Internet access to perform the exercises. We hope you enjoy them and that they make it easier for you to apply the techniques in real life.

You can learn more business analysis techniques by visiting the Business Analysis Learning Store at

(http://businessanalysisexperts.com/business-analysis-training-store/)

to see a wide selection of business analysis books, eCourses, virtual and face-to-face instructor-led training, as well as a selection of FREE Business Analysis training.

Meanwhile, please enjoy this book. We appreciate any comments, suggestions, recommended improvements, or complaints that you care to share with us. You can reach us via email at eBooks@businessanalysisexperts.com.

SETTING THE STAGE FOR WRITING EFFECTIVE REQUIREMENTS

Why Do You Need Better Requirements?

Look at the evolution of a typical business solution from the IT perspective. In the beginning, it all seems so simple. We think we know just what the customer wants (a bicycle), and we have a deadline, so let us get started.

Well, as we start to define the solution, we wonder whether the customer might need a little horsepower versus just "person-power" on this device, so maybe we should give it a motor.

Once we get into design, obviously, safety becomes a concern, so let us put a cage around it, and, of course, we will need some doors to get in and out.

There, is that not much better already? Now, developers love to try the latest and greatest technology, and to them, it is only reasonable that the customer might want to go off-road, like really, really fast, so why not give him the wings he deserves?

Finally, since nobody told the testers what to test for, their first test is to try the thing outside the atmosphere, which it would fail if the developers did not quickly attach external fuel tanks. Now, we are cooking with gas and ready to wow the customer with our whiz-bang solution. There is only one small problem, OOOOPS!

The customer wanted a simple kid's tricycle. Looks like we did not really grasp the situation, so while we are at it, we need to explain to our customer why we are 5,000,000% over budget and just a couple of centuries overdue.

What is the real problem here? Comprehension and communication, or rather, lack of both. Effectively captured and managed requirements could have avoided this entire mess.

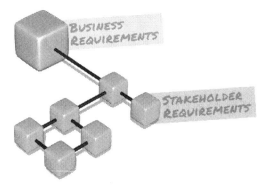

So what other good and great things would happen if we had effective, high-quality requirements?

The Benefits of Effective Requirements

⇨ **Higher return on technology investments**
You would expect to see a much better ROI (return on investment) for our development costs. Studies have shown that between a 2-1 and a 10-1 ROI is realistic on IT projects with the right parameters and effective requirements.

⇨ **Increased ability to realize business opportunities**
Actually, good requirements also improve the business community's ability to realize new business opportunities because IT is less busy reacting to the problems that bad requirements in previous releases created.

⇨ **Faster reaction to changing business situations**
If you base your software on good requirements, the business could also react more quickly to the evolving business environment.

⇨ **Decreased frustration and stress for all involved**
Better requirements would in turn reduce the levels of frustration and stress for everyone from the boardroom to the bathroom.

⇨ **Reduced misunderstandings in communication**
If the requirements were doing their job, they would improve communications among the stakeholders and thereby reduce misunderstandings.

⇨ **Business perspective has priority over technology**
Actually giving the business side priority over the technology side might sound like risky business from the IT perspective, but for the business community, this might actually right the ship and restore order to their world that has been lacking since we invented computers.

⇨ **Earlier delivery of business system**

⇨ **Fewer unneeded features**

⇨ **Lower defect rate**
Compared with all of the abovementioned benefits, the final 3 almost seem trivial, but, trust me, these three alone would easily pay for the time spent up front many times over.

Getting to these effective, high-quality requirements does appear to be non-trivial given that our industry has been struggling with this issue for decades.

What is the problem here? Why is it so difficult?

Managing Uncertainty

What you as the individual-responsible-for-defining-requirements are fighting is a little thing called the "Uncertainty Principle". If you happen to be knowledgeable about quantum physics, this may sound like old hat to you, but you may be surprised about our take on this. For normal people (i.e., us non-quantum-physicists), this definition of the uncertainty principle might even be understandable.

In the early days of any project, uncertainty may just be the only thing you have in abundance. The process of doing the project is actually one of reducing that uncertainty. Not to eliminate it, unfortunately, because that is impossible; there will always be some uncertainty. (According to a German saying, "Theory is when you know everything and nothing works. Reality is where everything works and you do not know why!") There will always be some uncertainty, some of which you are aware and some you do not even know about.

The real problem here is the pace at which the project reduces uncertainty. The green line shows how we expect uncertainty to drop.

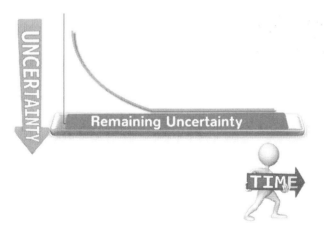

As you see, it drops very rapidly at the beginning (this is what we call the "analysis" phase) and then at some point starts to level off. At that point, further analysis is useless, so it is time to "Start Development".

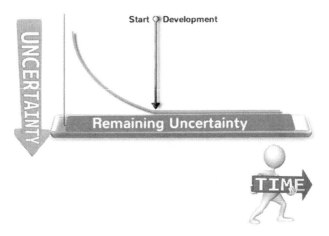

Obviously, uncertainty is now well contained and, if you try to reduce all uncertainty, you will be in analysis paralysis very quickly. Unfortunately, in the real world, the uncertainty curve looks much more like the red line.

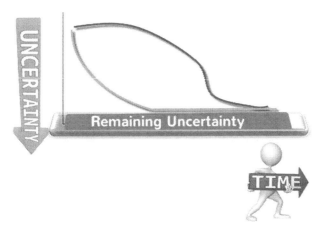

Note that at first, uncertainty does not drop; it increases. This represents what is happening at the beginning of the project when you thought you knew what the project would deliver. That is, until you started to do some analysis only to realize that what little you thought you knew was not even right! Now you have to figure out who to ask, how to ask it (and what to believe of the answers) before you can really get down to the nitty-gritty of nailing the requirements.

But wait, what's happening to our timeline here? Surely we can hold off starting development until we get the answers we need to do it right?

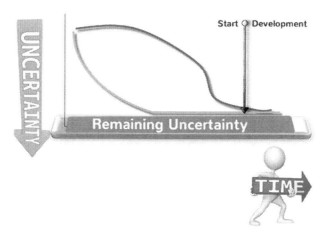

Sorry, but development cannot wait, they have a deadline to meet.

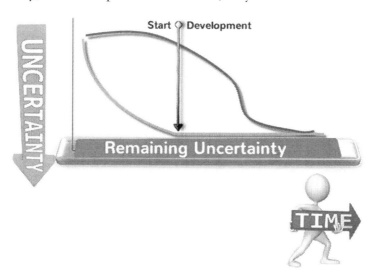

One of the oldest jokes in our industry is, "You go ask the customer what he wants and we will go ahead and start coding". Unfortunately, it seems to be as valid today as it was in the sixties when software was just coming of age. Nonetheless, instead of just complaining about the problems with defining requirements, we would like to suggest a solution.

What Do You Really Know?

We based our solution on a simple concept that says that all knowledge about the project falls into one of four basic categories. First off, there is what you know you know about the project, otherwise known as the "Facts". We realize that there are different levels of facts and differing degrees of certitude, but for the sake of simplicity, we will stick with our original title.

The next category represents what you know you do not know. Gosh, what do you call that? Well, we call it "Questions". If you can formulate a question, you are expressing something that you know you do not know. And, guess what? If someone would give you an answer to your question, you would have . . . that is right, **a new fact**.

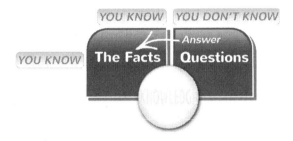

Of course, that assumes that the answer was from whoever has the knowledge and the authority (either alone is not enough) to answer the question. That leaves us with the lower half of our box.

First off, we have things that we do not know that we do know. HUH? How can you not know that you know something? Well, perhaps you did something in the past on other projects or in other lives that will help you on your current project; you just have not identified them yet. We call that category "Experience".

There is another category as well, that is something we call "Assumptions". Do you remember those questions we were just discussing? What happens if you cannot find anyone who has the authority and the knowledge to give you the answer? Maybe they are unavailable for your project or maybe nobody has ever tried to do what you are trying to do (at least within your organization).

At some point, you need an answer for every open question or someone somewhere will make an assumption and act upon it. That is life, and we are not saying there is anything wrong with it. We are simply pointing out that you need to get a better handle on it. If an assumption is necessary, make the most likely one and document it for posterity. Do not let it dangle or it will move quickly into the fourth dimension, which in our case is the final frontier.

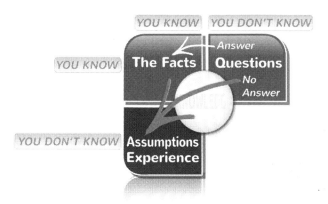

What you do not know that you do not know (or, as some prefer to call it, "the unknown unknowns") is what we call "Fate". Fate exists on every project, even the best run. As we mentioned earlier, there will always be things you do not know you do not know, so we have no choice but to live with it. It is, however, the number of factors that fall into this category that will ultimately determine the success or failure of your project.

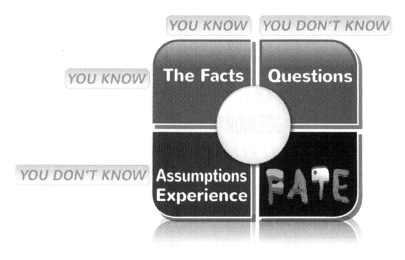

The challenge now has become, how can you manage

☑ what you know you know **and**

☑ keep track of what you know you do not know **while**

☑ using what you do not know you do know **to combat**

☑ what you do not know you do not know?

(If you can say that one three times without stuttering, you might be an analyst!)

THE Question File

Enter the Question File. The question file is one of the simplest forms of documentation for a project, but it just may be the most important document you create. All it needs to contain is a list of what you know you do not know.

Date	Question	Who	Answer	Date
12/3	What is the average age of human beings in the wild?			
12/5	Will manmade devices exceed the speed of light in our lifetime?			
12/7	Is there intelligent life on other planets?			
12/19	What's wrong with my golf swing?			

Try to express the question in a manner that any answer you get becomes a new fact. I recommend dating each question so that you can keep track of when you realized on the project that you needed to know something and did not.

The "Who" column is where you can jot down who within your organization you feel has the knowledge and the authority to answer the question, either by name or by role/job title. This may change; it is not cast in concrete. You just think that this person would be your most likely target for getting an answer at this time.

In the "Answer" column, you can document whatever you get for an answer. Just in case you do not get an answer by the time you need it, you can also document your assumptions here. Just make sure that you document that it is an assumption and, by the way, I recommend telling the world (or at least anyone who you think maybe should have given you the answer) about your assumed answer.

As a technique, you might consider a simple email that says, "I needed to know this and since we have not been able to get a definitive answer to date, we are going to work under the assumption that . . ."

The final "Date" column is to document when you got the answer (or made the assumption).

Date	Question	Who	Answer	Date
12/3	1 What is the average age of human beings in the wild?	Genome Project Leader	35 Years	12/8
12/5	2 Will manmade devices exceed the speed of light in our lifetime?	Arthur C. Clark		
12/7	3 Is there intelligent life on other planets?	???	**Assumption:** Yes, based on math	12/31
12/19	4 What's wrong with my golf swing?	Tiger Woods		

Now, if you had a question file for your project, you could perform magic tricks. Just for example, you could sort your file on the "Answer" column and count how many questions you had answered and how many were still open. The ratio of the two shows you where you are on the uncertainty curve I mentioned earlier.

You could also sort the file on the "Who" column to determine who you should be interviewing next (maybe the person for whom you have the most open questions? Hint, hint.).

If you browsed this file and compared the date you identified the question with the date you got a response, it might even tell you something about the priority of the project from the perspective of the "Who" column. Finally, if someone new comes on to the project, it could just be invaluable as a tool for getting them up to speed quickly and without you spending time telling them everything that is in the file. As I said, it is simply magic.

Date	Question	Who	Answer
12/3	What is the average age of human beings in the wild?	Genome Project Leader	35 Years
12/5	Will manmade devices exceed the speed of light in our lifetime?	Arthur C. Clark	
12/7	Is there intelligent life on other planets?	???	
12/19	What's wrong with my golf swing?	Tiger Woods	

Now, we have told you a lot about the problems and challenges that plague good requirements gathering efforts, but that is just preaching. It is time for you to experience the challenge yourself.

Exercise: The Subjectivity of Language

All exercises in this book are optional. They are online exercises that take anywhere from a few minutes to 20 minutes.

This exercise will make you aware of how challenging effective communication can be.

I have a problem with my mouse

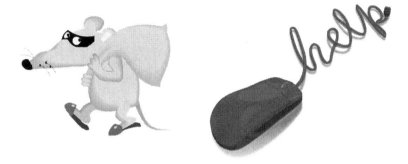

The English language, and any other language for that matter, is very subjective, meaning that the meaning of a word or phrase depends heavily on context. This subjectivity leads to problems on IT projects but it can even be challenging in normal life. I have a little exercise to demonstrate my point. I would like you to complete an assignment but to do that you may need additional information.

Type any questions you can think of in the text area provided. When you run out of questions, press the submit button to see what awaits you.

To start the exercise, please go to http://goo.gl/4ApiUf

(DISCLAIMER: If you attempt the exercises on a standard PC, please use IE10 or higher or Chrome. They may not work on FireFox.)

The "Real" Problem with Requirements

As you can now appreciate, to clarify requirements, you need to make sure that you understand the intent and not just the words because human languages are rich in ambiguity. This problem only gets worse when you start cross-cultural discussions, even with someone with whom you share the language.

I would like to illustrate that with a true story. A colleague of mine went "down under" (a.k.a. Australia) a few years ago to teach a business analysis course. One of her endearing traits was a burning desire to ensure that her students were comfortable with the pace and topics being covered. Her method for asking that was to query the group regularly and one of her favorite phrases was, "Are we all happy campers?"

When she tried this the first time in Australia, she got a couple of strange looks and giggles but little else. Later, she asked it once again and, again, the result was not what she expected. Something was definitely wrong, but what? During a break, one of the students explained that the term "happy camper" in Australia referred to gays, and the group was wondering why my colleague was constantly polling them for their sexual preferences.

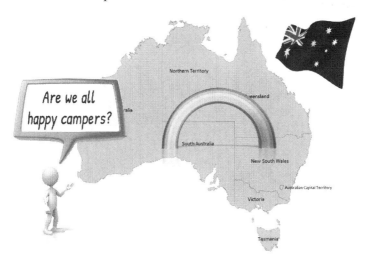

This is a prime example of what can happen when we cross cultural boundaries. However, do not feel complacent just because you stay in

these United States. In any given corporation, I can guarantee you that different groups interpret a common term differently. A common example is the term "Account". Just ask a salesperson and an accountant to define what that term means.

The real problem is, of course, the ambiguity and subjectivity of our language that I mentioned earlier. If you ask a subject matter expert what he or she wants "the system" to do, you will get all kinds of different responses. You will get fragments of thoughts, subjective and ill-defined terms and terminology, words and phrases that are ambiguous and (just to add a little variety) concepts and wishes that could change in a heartbeat.

Of course, this only becomes a challenge when it is necessary for various groups to communicate with each other. Since folks in the IT world typically have to communicate with everyone else in the known universe, it is here at the latest that such miscommunication becomes a major issue.

To develop a technology solution to business problems, we need to have clearly defined requirements that are not subject to anyone's interpretation (good luck on that) and that are objectively measurable.

We do not want to leave the task of deciding what the subject matter experts want up to the developers. We tried that back in the '60s. We tried it again in the '70s, the '80s, the '90s. It never has worked! The business community needs to be in control of what the business wants to do. IT is a supporting function and exists to support the needs and wants of the business community.

Online resources for you:

⇨ FREE video: What Are Requirements?
http://businessanalysisexperts.com/product/what-are-business-requirements-stakeholder-solution/

⇨ FREE video: An Overview of Business Analysis for Information Technology
http://businessanalysisexperts.com/product/what-is-business-analysis-overview-it/

⇨ FREE video: An Introduction to Business Analysis Techniques
http://businessanalysisexperts.com/product/business-analysis-techniques/

⇨ If you prefer videos, this book in eCourse format
http://businessanalysisexperts.com/product/video-course-writing-requirements/

⇨ Software Requirements Are A Communication Problem
http://www.allaboutagile.com/software-requirements-are-a-communication-problem/

⇨ Understanding the root causes of poor software requirements
https://blogs.msdn.microsoft.com/nickmalik/2009/02/18/understanding-the-root-causes-of-poor-software-requirements/

⇨ Business, User, and System Requirement
http://enfocussolutions.com/business-user-and-system-requirements/

⇨ 8 Characteristics of good user requirements
http://www.slideshare.net/guest24d72f/8-characteristics-of-good-user-requirements-presentation

⇨ How To Prevent The Negative Impacts Of Poor Requirements
https://www.batimes.com/articles/how-to-prevent-the-negative-impacts-of-poor-requirements.html

CAPTURING REQUIREMENTS

This chapter will help you:

⇨ Reduce Complexity and Increase Comprehension
⇨ Develop Well-structured Requirement Statements
⇨ Consider the Business Result, Not the IT Solution

We have established that expressing business needs in a manner that solution providers (i.e., developers, testers, etc.) can really understand is a non-trivial undertaking. So where do you start?

We suggest that it is extremely difficult if you try to write perfect requirements from the get-go. Our process is one of capturing requirements in any way, shape or form as quickly as possible. Once you have captured them, take the time to morph them into the form that the solution providers need.

The time you save later on the project by avoiding misinterpretation and confusion will more than make up for any time you spend up front ensuring that your requirements are as good as they can possibly be.

In this section we introduce the first two of our four simple rules for writing effective requirements.

Follow the KISS concept

Our first rule sounds simple enough and, as all good rules are, it is!

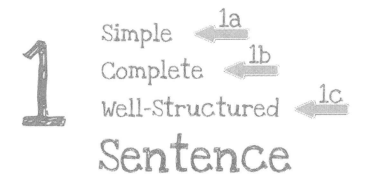

This rule states that each individual requirement should be a simple, complete, well-structured sentence. That does not sound very difficult, does it? Well, in theory, life is simple (it is, after all, just another four-letter word); it is living that makes it complicated.

Let us take a slightly more in-depth look at rule 1. Since we designed this Book for anyone wearing the BA hat, meaning anyone who defines requirements, we will follow a time-honored tradition of analysis called decomposition.

There are three distinct components to rule 1:

1. **Simple**
2. **Complete**
3. **Well-structured**

We are going to look at each individual component to figure out why it is important and how each part contributes to the whole.

Reducing Complexity Increases Comprehension

A "good" Business Requirement is a simple sentence, meaning it

> ☑ states one thing and states it well
>
> ☑ is not a compound sentence (and, or, but, …)
>
> ☑ avoids the use of limiting phrases (unless, except, . . .)

A requirement should be a simple sentence that states **only one thing**. However, it should do a good job at that. If you try to express too much in a single sentence, you actually lose clarity.

For instance, the sentence,

"The user will navigate to the coverage screen, enter personal and vehicle data, and submit the application"

---

contains **three** distinct thoughts. It would be clearer if you expressed each thought separately, e.g.:

---

1. "The user will navigate to the coverage screen"

2. "The user will enter personal and vehicle data"

3. "The user will submit the application"

By the way, compound sentences are, by definition, never simple. That means, you should not have "if, ands or buts" in your requirement.

Actually, you have to take that with a grain of salt. The word "and" is a phenomenally versatile word in the English language and, in my experience, in any language. It can be a sign of a compound sentence - if the sentence contains two phrases each of which contains an action (verb) and a subject or object (nouns). The other use of the word "and" is to create a list of items grouped together based on like characteristics. Here is an example of what we mean.

The requirement,

"The user will select coverage types **and** the system will calculate the premium based on vehicle values and driving record"

is a **compound sentence.** Many people have to read the sentence several times to understand what it really says. It is much easier to understand the two simple sentences,

1. "The user will select coverage types" and

2. "The system will calculate the premium based on vehicle values **and** driving record."

Note that, in the last example, the "and" is used to create a list (vehicle values and driving record), not a compound sentence. Expressed this way, each requirement statement is truly a simple sentence that expresses one thing and expresses it well.

We also recommend against using delimiting qualifiers such as "unless" or "except" in the requirement. These typically indicate an exception, which you can express much better as a separate and distinct requirement (as you see in our next example).

The requirement,

"A temporary proof of insurance will be issued **unless** the customer has bad credit"

Breaking this statement down into two distinct sentences, one addressing the "norm", (we hope, good credit) and the other specifically addressing the exception (bad credit) makes it much easier to understand and less likely to be misinterpreted.

1. "The system should issue a temporary proof of insurance for customers with good credit"

2. "The system should reject applications from customers with bad credit"

In summary,

A Complete Sentence Forces a Complete Thought

A "good" Business Requirement is a **complete** sentence, meaning it

- ☑ does not depend on other sources of information
- ☑ contains subject, verb, object and appropriate modifiers

A complete sentence does not depend on other sources of information (as much as humanly possible). Why is that important? Well, if I give you a bullet or fragment of a requirement, I am leaving it up to you to "fill in the blanks". The biggest problem of course is that different people will "fill in the blanks" differently, which, in fact destroys any chance of effective communication.

For example,

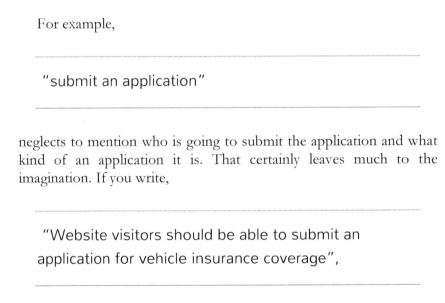

"submit an application"

neglects to mention who is going to submit the application and what kind of an application it is. That certainly leaves much to the imagination. If you write,

"Website visitors should be able to submit an application for vehicle insurance coverage",

there is much less room for interpretation and conjecture.

The second half of this rule, referring to the subject, verb, object, and appropriate modifiers, is really an extension of that. Someone, somewhere down the line can (and probably will) misinterpret anything that you leave open to interpretation.

For example, the phrase

"customer has good standing"

---

is certainly missing significant information that the reader will have to supply in order to make sense of the statement. As human beings, we are very capable of inventing an interpretation and then firmly believing that it is the correct interpretation regardless of whether the original author verifies it.

A more complete version of "customer has good standing" would be,

---

Customers who are current in their payments for existing policies are considered customers in good standing.

Structured Requirement Statements

A "good" Business Requirement is a well-structured sentence, meaning it either:

- ☑ identifies an actor and describes what the actor should (or should not) do
- ☑ OR is an external constraint that must be enforced

This dimension of rule 1 is not simple because it deals with the structure of a requirement statement. First off, it recommends that a good business requirement starts with an actor, which is either a specific role or a specific department/division (or "the system"), and indicates something that the actor "should" or "should not" do.

For example, instead of writing,

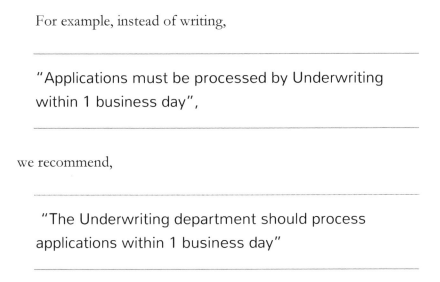

"Applications must be processed by Underwriting within 1 business day",

we recommend,

"The Underwriting department should process applications within 1 business day"

as a well-structured requirement.

Incidentally, this rule is not without contention. Others maintain you should always state the requirement in the form that includes the verb "will" or "will not" based on the theory that it is impossible to test a requirement that contains the verb "should". We agree with that philosophy. The contention is around the point in the life cycle of a requirement at which you determine if it is a "Must" or a "Should".

If you express all Requirements using the verb "will" from the get-go, you are actually precluding a later prioritization of the requirements. If every requirement has the verb "will", then "obviously" the solution has to deliver all of them, meaning they are all "Musts". While you are in the very early stages of gathering requirements, it is much more important to express the fact that you do not know whether the solution will or will not include this particular requirement.

Ergo, we recommend the use of the verb "should" during the requirements elicitation phase and waiting until requirements prioritization to distinguish the "Musts".

The major exception to this rule is a situation in which the Requirement actually represents a constraint, which designates a condition (or state or behavior or component or feature) that is externally mandated. That implies that no one on the project team up to and including the project sponsor has the authority to change it. Your project team has no choice in the matter, ergo, express the constraint with the absolute "must" (or "must not"). For instance,

---

"The UPS truck arrives daily at 10:30 am"

---

is not as good as

"The mail clerk must have all packages ready for UPS pickup at 10:30 am".

Written this way, the constraint focuses on how it affects an actor of our system, meaning the mail clerk.

I think we have talked enough about rule 1. It is time to put your understanding of this concept to the test.

Exercise: Simple, Complete, and Well-Structured

All exercises in this book are optional. They are online exercises that take anywhere from a few minutes to 20 minutes.

This exercise will test your interpretation of Rule 1.

In this exercise, you are going to test how well our first rule works on a set of requirement fragments or statements. For each presented requirement statement, you have to decide whether you think it is a simple sentence, a complete sentence, and / or a well-structured sentence. Each presented statement can meet one, two, all, or none of these restrictions. As you go through the exercise, we will offer guidance as to whether we agree with your choices.

To start the exercise, please go to http://goo.gl/ddCwP3

(DISCLAIMER: If you attempt the exercises on a standard PC, please use IE10 or higher or Chrome. They may not work on FireFox.)

Define the Business Need

All right, now that you know about the importance of simple, complete well-structured sentences, let us add a second rule. This is a rule that has caused analysts fits at least since the '70s when we first started thinking about what requirements are and why they are important. It is the old "What-not-how" rule.

What this rule is trying to get across is that you need to keep the technology out of the picture until you have a good grasp of what the business community needs (or wants).

For those of us who grew up in the IT world, this is really a lot harder than it may seem. First off, we generally love technology or we would not have gotten involved with computers at the level of detail we need to be to be successful developers, designers, and whatnot. I include myself in this group since I was a developer for several years and I can relate to the challenge.

Secondly, the latest wiz-bang gizmos that our industry has a habit of throwing at us every couple of months excites many of us in IT and we want to try them out as soon as possible. They always seem to promise to solve the very problem we were just struggling with on the last project but their solution is so much more elegant, we just have to try it. Recognize that every solution creates its own set of problems. Before you try to sell your decision makers on the power of the latest and greatest technology, you really ought to make sure that you understand the business needs.

So let us look at what this ubiquitous "what-not-how" rule is really all about.

Consider the Business Result, Not the IT Solution

A "good" requirement emphasizes "**what**" should be done or "what" the end result should be, not "**how**" to do it by:

- ☑ avoiding preconceived solutions

- ☑ describing business logic (rules) instead of a technology solution

- ☑ expressing the destination, not the journey

Primarily, it is about focusing on the business results and avoiding thinking about how to achieve them. Avoiding preconceived notions seems like a great idea, but all too often, we go into a project with blinders on, thinking that what the customer wants (needs, really) is better automation. If only you had the right technology, this whole project would be a snap.

Going back to my previous statement that every solution creates its own set of problems, the business community can testify to the fact that the last technological innovation that we suggested caused the current problems. As a result, the subject matter experts might have a justifiable degree of skepticism as to why today's technology is so much better than the technology they finally got working after so many hiccups and false starts.

Another way of avoiding the solution trap is to think about the destination (that would be the "what") without contemplating "how" I can get there given my parameters. Here is an example.

Let us say I have scheduled a class in Houston next Thursday and Friday. The class starts at 8:30 AM and I have to be at the customer site at 8 AM to set everything up.

In that context, being at the customer site at 8 AM Thursday morning is my business requirement. I could fly there on Wednesday and stay overnight in a hotel (as most civilized folk would probably do). I could drive there in my motorhome or even hitchhike from Tampa, Florida if I feel lucky and relish the added element of uncertainty.

Houston

8:00 AM
Thursday morning   Tampa

The point is, there are many possible ways of satisfying the business need, so do not get hung up on the 'obvious' solution too soon.

Here is a real example to clarify exactly how subtle the difference can be. If my SME tells me that she has a problem with customers entering illegal state abbreviations in the address box of a form, my question might be,

> *"Why do you not offer them a drop-down box to choose their state? That way, you would never get an illegal state abbreviation?"*

What is wrong with my question? The drop-down box is a technology. Not necessarily a bad one, by the way, but not necessarily the best either. If instead of jumping to the solution, I consider what the SME is really trying to achieve, I might write a requirement stating,

"The customer should provide a valid state abbreviation."

That expresses the business needs without specifying HOW I am going to achieve it. All right, now it is your turn to try this rule out.

Exercise: Avoiding the Elusive "How"

All exercises in this book are optional. They are online exercises that take anywhere from a few minutes to 20 minutes.

This exercise will test your interpretation of Rule 2.

We modified the requirements in this exercise to comply with Rule 1. The challenge is whether we agree on how well they comply with the "what-not-how" rule. Your first decision is going to be whether you accept the statement as OK or would recommend a revision. If you choose the latter, enter your recommended revision in the presented text box. After that, we will present our recommendations as an example of our thinking.

To start the exercise, please go to http://goo.gl/RU7tzC

(DISCLAIMER: If you attempt the exercises on a standard PC, please use IE10 or higher or Chrome. They may not work on FireFox.)

Online resources for you:

Are you working in an Agile Environment?
Watch the following FREE videos:

⇨ FREE video: Business Analysis Using User Stories
http://youtu.be/NzSsE37opB0

⇨ FREE video: Keep Your User Story Simple
http://youtu.be/WzUgcHYTbqA

⇨ FREE video: A User Story Expresses the What, Not the How
http://youtu.be/CdnNwBKTOHA

More online resources:

⇨ Good Requirements Deliver a High ROI
http://enfocussolutions.com/good-requirements-deliver-a-high-roi/

⇨ Writing Good Requirements
http://homepages.laas.fr/kader/Hooks.pdf

⇨ Agile Requirements: Not An Oxymoron
https://www.batimes.com/articles/agile-requirements-not-an-oxymoron.html

⇨ 15 Tips for Writing Better Requirements
http://businessanalystlearnings.com/blog/2013/7/26/15-tips-for-writing-better-requirements

REQUIREMENTS AND PROJECT SCOPE

This chapter will help you:

⇨ Enforce Your Project Scope
⇨ Define Requirements Scope at the Component Level
⇨ Focus Requirements and Minimize Misinterpretations
⇨ Identify Relevant Requirements

That gets us through the first two rules.

We now know that a good business requirement is a simple, complete, and well-structured sentence that states one thing and states it well. It should not be a compound sentence or be missing anything necessary to make sense of it and it does not contain embedded exceptions. We also noted that well-structured means that it starts with an actor (like "the role / system / department") should (or should not), unless it is a constraint.

Our second rule ensures that the requirement is a true business requirement, meaning it focuses on the business outcome as opposed to the technology used to achieve the outcome.

Keep Your Requirements in Scope

Rule 3 states that a requirement has to target one or more solution **components** that are **in scope** for your project.

3 Targets Components that are in Scope

This is what we call relevance. You might have a perfectly good requirement statement that is well structured, simple, etc. but unless it actually describes something your project can affect, it is certainly not an effective requirement. This deals with whether your requirement expresses some behavior or feature of a solution component over which you have control. Before we look at rule 3 in more detail, we have to clarify this "scope" thing.

The Project Scope Statement

Obviously, without a reliable definition of the scope of your project, you do not have a defined project. What you might have is a project that determines what the scope of a future project could be. We typically refer to this type of a project as a "preliminary study" or something similar. The scope statement clearly delineates your project from the environment of the organization by establishing the boundaries for your project.

It typically specifies functions, departments/divisions, roles/job titles, etc. that the project could affect or influence. Quite often, the specification is, however, subject to interpretation and deciding whether a specific solution component is in or out of scope can require some imagination.

As a good practice, consider listing components of the solution that you will specifically exclude. Since this category theoretically encompasses everything that is not in scope, you might ask why this is necessary. Experience teaches that if there is a potential for a specific component to be in scope but you have consciously decided to exclude it, you should document this fact as part of the scope statement to avoid future discussions and misconceptions.

We have here an example of a scope statement, which you will need in the upcoming exercise.

> **SCOPE STATEMENT**
>
> This project will enhance our web-based Policy Maintenance System by allowing policyholders to interact directly with their insurance policies or claims. The system will support web-based policy payments and allow prospects to apply for temporary coverage pending underwriting rate approval."

As a side note, the author of this gem is your project sponsor, the manager of the underwriting department.

Since requirements are supposed to define (in some manner) components that will become a future business solution, we need to reach agreement on just what those components are. You cannot build a house without the building blocks. In the IT universe, we call the blocks we need to build a business solution 'components'.

Reality is that every solution consists of some common components, but we need to understand just what that means. In the best tradition of analysis anywhere, the best way to figure this out is to take this thing called a "business information system" apart and look at the pieces.

So, just what are the components of a business information system?

Exercise: Relevant Requirement Components

All exercises in this book are optional. They are online exercises that take anywhere from a few minutes to 20 minutes.

This exercise will test your ability to brainstorm common components of a business solution containing an IT application.

We will let you ponder this. When you have identified all the components you can, we will compare your perspective to our perspective to establish a common baseline. Please list any components you can think of in the text area provided.

To start the exercise, please go to http://goo.gl/ckEdhX

(DISCLAIMER: If you attempt the exercises on a standard PC, please use IE10 or higher or Chrome. They may not work on FireFox.)

Combat Scope Creep from the Start

So now that you know what scope and components are, let us get back to rule 3 and look at it in more detail.

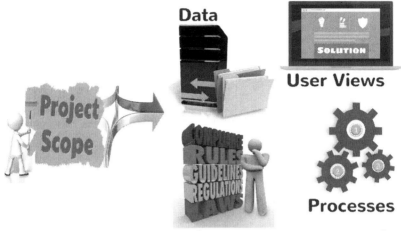

A "focused" requirement statement **targets** specific components, meaning it defines:

☑ a desired behavior (or function) of one or more components (**functional requirement**)

☑ **OR** a feature of one or more components of your solution that you can control (**non-functional requirement**)

It should never try to do both. Here is a for instance:

We have revised a requirement to fit our first two rules so that it reads,

---

"The system should *calculate collision premiums* based on replacement value of the vehicle including applicable SALES TAXES."

At first glance, it might appear to focus only on one component, namely the collision premium. Looking closer, however, we see that it actually defines two distinct dimensions: it defines a *function* (calculate collision premium) and defines a FEATURE of a second component, namely the inclusion of sales taxes in the replacement value. Make it easier to understand and to manage by splitting it into the two relevant requirements, one focusing on the function, and the other focusing on the feature, as in

Functional Requirement

1. *"The system should calculate collision premiums based on the replacement value of the vehicle. "*

Non-functional Requirement

2. "THE REPLACEMENT VALUE OF THE VEHICLE SHOULD INCLUDE APPLICABLE SALES TAXES. "

Both of these statements are still simple, complete, well-structured sentences that emphasize the what, not the how, but beyond that, each now focuses on one specific behavior or feature of one or more components of the future solution.

Why is this important? The way the original statement reads, I do not know if the "applicable sales taxes" relate to the collision premium or the replacement value. The separation clarifies the relationship.

Relevant Requirements Reduce Project Effort

All right, so assuming your requirement is component-focused, is it in scope for your project? Rule 3 implies that a "relevant" business requirement is in scope for your project, meaning:

☑ you have the authority to change or replace all components / behaviors / states / features to implement the requirement

☑ the changes you implement do not impact other components that are out of scope

For instance,

"The system should calculate premiums based on the current rates as ratified by the state insurance board."

Might sound perfectly good as a component-focused requirement, but there are two distinct components referenced.

One of them (the calculate premium function) is certainly in scope or you cannot do your project whereas the second (the ratification process) is probably out of scope since it is outside your organization's control.

Not Scoped	Scoped
The system should calculate premiums based on the current rates as ratified by the state insurance board.	• IN: The system should calculate premiums based on the current rates. • OUT: Rates are ratified by the state insurance board.

Furthermore, the changes you implement should not affect any component that is not specifically in scope. If you change a behavior of a component that is in scope and that change causes a component that is out of scope to change, that inadvertently increases the scope of your project (a phenomenon we generally refer to as scope creep).

Here is a good example.

"The system will report premium receipts daily to Accounting where they will be posted to the general ledger"

Assuming that the posting to GL is not part of your project, you should rephrase this statement to read:

"The system will report premium receipts daily to Accounting."

This requirement could be legitimate as a constraint imposed by the Accounting department. You should also note that Accounting posting premium receipts to the general ledger (or anything else they do with it) is out of scope for your project.

Identifying Relevant Requirements

So, how do we go about determining the relevance of a requirement?

First step, take the time to contemplate which specific components the requirement could affect. You can use the list of potential components from the last exercise to help you figure out what those components might be.

people	business rules	process
data	organization	training
test environment	methodology	hardware
software	networks	communications
databases	help desks	security
documentation	user manuals	design
reports	programs	modules
files	inputs	outputs

Once you have the list of components, you need a scope statement.

Once you have a scope statement and identified potential solution components, the challenge is to determine whether, in your humble opinion (actually, the opinion of your project sponsor and other team members) each named component or specified behavior in some manner can contribute to achieving the project objective AND whether you can affect it. If so, declare that part of the requirement to be in scope, otherwise it is out.

As a side note, if putting the component out of scope leads to considerable discussion before your group comes to consensus, specify the component in your "Out of Scope" list. Remember, knowing what specifically is OUT of scope (and why) can be just as important as knowing what is IN scope.

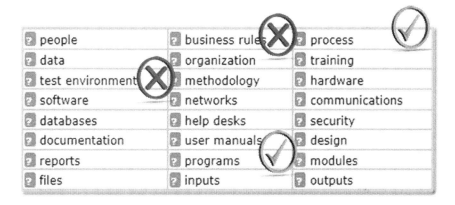

people	business rules	process
data	organization	training
test environment	methodology	hardware
software	networks	communications
databases	help desks	security
documentation	user manuals	design
reports	programs	modules
files	inputs	outputs

I do not know whether it is just me, but that certainly sounded like it is time for an exercise to test this theory.

Exercise: Testing the Scope Boundaries

All exercises in this book are optional. They are online exercises that take anywhere from a few minutes to 20 minutes.

This exercise will test your ability to check your requirements for their relevance to your project.

At this point, we have improved our requirements, but are they relevant? That is the question, and this is a neat little exercise to give you an opportunity to test once again whether you agree with us. You will have to identify components first, and then for the second step identifying which are in and out of scope.

To start the exercise, please go to http://goo.gl/zLUAmd

(DISCLAIMER: If you attempt the exercises on a standard PC, please use IE10 or higher or Chrome. They may not work on FireFox.)

Recap of Rules One through Three

You now own three of our four basic rules for writing effective requirement statements. Since the fourth rule is broader and more complex, we would like to ensure that you have a firm grasp of these three before we broach the topic of ambiguity.

To recap the first three rules:

Rule 1 states that you start by writing simple, complete, well-structured sentences that state one thing and state it well. Avoid compound sentences and do not use limiting phrases. Write independent, role- or constraint-focused sentences that contain all of the relevant components and pertinent information.

As per Rule 2, good requirements emphasize what is needed from a business perspective, not how to use technology, so avoid preconceived solutions by describing the outcome or destination, not the trip.

Rule 3 is designed to ensure that each requirement statement focuses on behaviors or features of specific components of the solution and the entire requirement statement in scope of your project, meaning your project team has the authority to implement it.

Given that information, it is time for a "mid-term" exam to test your application of these three simple rules. As always, we will provide feedback to your answers to each requirement, so go for it! We will continue the class with Rule four when you are done.

<u>Exercise</u>: Applying the First Three Rules

All exercises in this book are optional. They are online exercises that take anywhere from a few minutes to 20 minutes.

This exercise will test your ability to evaluate requirements for compliance with all of the rules we have covered.

We are going to present you with a scope statement and several requirements from an entirely different project. Your assignment is to determine whether each requirement complies with each rule. As a recommended approach, check each requirement one rule at a time and if it violates any part of the rule, move on to the next requirement. Check the box only if the requirement meets all parts of the rule.

To start the exercise, please go to http://goo.gl/s5I1aR

(DISCLAIMER: If you attempt the exercises on a standard PC, please use IE10 or higher or Chrome. They may not work on FireFox.)

Online resources for you:

Are you working in an Agile Environment?
Watch the following FREE videos:

⇨ Writing User Stories that Are In Scope of Your Project
http://youtu.be/vbq_ARZRyKM

More online resources:

⇨ Project And Solution Scope - The Importance Of Both!
http://www.batimes.com/angela-wick/project-and-solution-scope-the-importance-of-both.html

⇨ Creating a Project Scope Statement
http://www.free-management-ebooks.com/faqpm/scope-05.htm

⇨ Scope Management Plan Checklist
http://www.free-management-ebooks.com/dldchk/dlchpm-scope.htm

⇨ Documenting the Project Requirements
http://www.free-management-ebooks.com/faqpm/scope-04.htm

⇨ How Should a Business Analyst Define Project Scope?
http://www.corpedgroup.com/resources/ba/HowShouldBADefineScope.asp

⇨ Project scope and requirements management
http://www.slideshare.net/tictactoe123/project-scope-and-requirements-management

⇨ FREE Business Analysis Videos
http://businessanalysisexperts.com/product-category/free-business-analysis-training/

FINDING AND FIXING
AMBIGUOUS REQUIREMENTS

This chapter will help you:

- ➪ Uncover Ambiguity Using Desk-Checking
- ➪ Restate Requirements to Remove Ambiguity
- ➪ Pick the Right Peers for Requirements Review
- ➪ Revise, Define and Clarify Your Requirements

Ambiguity Kills Projects!

Why you might ask? Often, those tasked with delivering the solution do not know whether their solution meets the customer's needs until they have developed it. On the other side, the business community does not know what they are going to get until the developers demonstrate the new system. Misunderstood, ambiguous, and assumption-laden requirements cause more project failures than any other single factor. Study after study confirms that simple fact.

Unless all participants involved in the process of planning, defining, designing, developing, validating and delivering the technology understand the intent of the requirements, your IT projects are at high risk of failure. According to periodic studies by the Standish Group, a high percentage of all IT projects fail and the majority of them fail due to problems with the requirements.

Why is this such an intractable challenge?

Who Needs to Understand Your Requirements?

One of the major problems that you face on IT projects lies in the number of people who have to understand what a requirement says – and what it does not say – in order for the project to be successful. You have to make sure that your requirements are understandable and clear to all of the various groups that you are dealing with as a business analyst. You have to think about what the requirement means to all groups.

For starters, do all of your users agree on what it means? You usually have to talk with several different stakeholders to get the full picture of what they as a group want or need the solution to do. Quite often, this leads to inconsistent or unclear statements that you have to help them clarify.

Next, make sure that you and the users agree on what the requirement means. If you were the developer of the system, you would be done now. However, if you are an analyst then you are simply a translator in this context, so the game is not over yet.

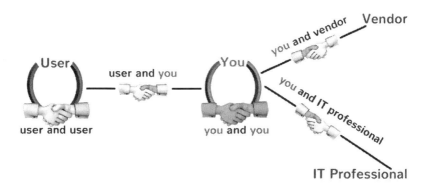

If you decide to have the solution built in-house, you have to communicate your requirements to an IT professional or developer and make sure that that person understands your requirements well enough to be able to do his or her job.

If you outsource the development, your IT vendor has to understand the requirements correctly. If the vendor wants to offer a bid to solve your business problem, you would like to make sure that the solution they offer meets your needs. That means that they have to understand the requirement as well as you do.

The key is to make all involved parties understand and agree upon the requirements before buying or building the solution.

Of course, the challenge is that you are dealing with people, each with his or her own background, culture, and (in today's international marketplace) possibly language. Navigating these muddy waters of communication can be so challenging that it might also mean that you have to test yourself to make sure you know what each requirement means and that you can communicate it at the appropriate level of detail to each different target audience.

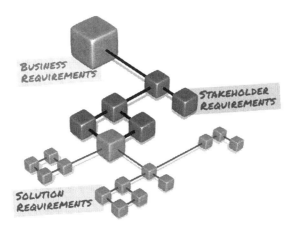

Roadblocks to Effective Requirements

Unfortunately, that is not as simple as it sounds. Here is the problem in real life. The author of a requirement knows what it means. It seems so simple, they think that the rest of the world should "get it" right away.

For instance, assume you are the manager of inventory acquisition in an organization. Your job is to purchase enough of each product to be able to meet future customer demand but avoid having more on hand than is necessary to avoid tying up too much capital in inventory. When someone wearing the BA hat asks you what you want your future Automated Product Replenishment (APR) system to do, you might simply say something like,

Well, for starters, we need a forecast

When asked to explain what you mean, you might expand on your statement by saying,

---

"The system should predict the amount of stuff we will sell"

This requirement actually meets the first three rules that we reviewed earlier. So what could possibly be unclear about it?

The Challenge to Understanding

If you are going to improve the understandability of a requirement, the first thing you need to do is identify which words or phrases might be ambiguous or easily misunderstood.

Contemplate the stated requirement,

"The system should predict the amount of stuff
we will sell"

⬦ First off, the word "stuff" could mean just about anything you want it to mean. When the developers read it, they will most likely make an assumption.

⬦ How accurate do you expect the "amount" of the prediction to be, in individual items, cases, palettes, or truckloads?

⬦ When you say "system", are you implying that you expect the automated system to predict sales totally without human intervention? Is it possible that there will be some manual involvement in the process?

⬦ What time span does the forecast cover, the rest of your life, until tomorrow afternoon, next week, or until the company goes out of business?

As you can see, although this simple, complete, and well-structured sentence seems very good, it still has many potential meanings. The fact that different people could interpret the requirement differently is what makes our life difficult. Before you can do anything to improve your requirements, you need to recognize potential areas for misunderstanding.

Rule 4 is the focus of this and the next chapter. It specifically states that an effective requirement statement is

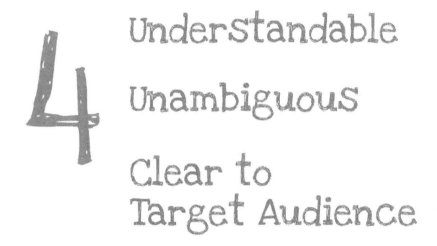

which includes both the business and the IT community.

Desk-Checking Uncovers Ambiguity

The challenge you face is how to identify words or phrases that might be subject to misinterpretation. How can you misunderstand words when you wrote them? If you did not understand them, you probably would not have written them.

The easiest way to get started is by simply re-reading the requirement statements you wrote and make a conscious effort to misunderstand them.

John went to the bank

To get the biggest effect from this "desk checking" exercise, we recommend performing the critical review in a different environment than the one in which you wrote the statements. For instance, if you wrote the requirements in the morning, review them in the afternoon (or vice versa). If you wrote them at your desk, review them at home or on your commute. By changing the time or the physical environment, you might change your perception of what you wrote.

Once you have completed this step, you might think that you have a perfectly understandable requirement statement, but what do others think? The next person that you need to reach agreement with regarding the meaning of the words is the subject matter expert (SME). We have here an exercise that will help you see the process of getting unclear requirements clarified through the SME.

Exercise: Finding Ambiguity with the SME

All exercises in this book are optional. They are online exercises that take anywhere from a few minutes to 20 minutes.

This exercise will test your ability to identify ambiguous terms in a requirement statement.

In this exercise, you will see a requirement and a button for viewing background information. After familiarizing yourself with the background, read the requirement to identify words or phrases that need clarification. Point + click to select the questionable content then drag and drop it onto to the SME to get her reaction. Try it out! Our SME might be an electronic avatar but she is quite knowledgeable.

Click the "Submit Answers" button to see the SME's clarifications of terms we consider ambiguous.

To start the exercise, please go to http://goo.gl/syFqX1

(DISCLAIMER: If you attempt the exercises on a standard PC, please use IE10 or higher or Chrome. They may not work on FireFox.)

Use Peer Reviews to Increase Understandability

Since requirements are the primary tool of communication between the business community and the technology team (and they form the foundation of a future IT solution), you might want to run them by a colleague, a peer, your manager, or even a developer to get their take.

Given that you are trying to communicate business needs to a technical audience, it would be great if that technical audience understood not just the words but also the meaning of the requirement.

Now, if someone gives you a simple, single, English sentence and asks you if you understand it, what are you going to say? Assuming that you are honest (and willing to work with the other person), you would most likely consider the sentence to see if it generates any questions or throws any red flags in your mind. If not, you are most likely going to say, "Sure. It makes sense to me". The author can now walk away, feeling that the requirement is perfectly understandable.

In this scenario, how do either of you know whether you understood the same thing under the sentence?

Restating Requirements to Find Ambiguity

One of the best ways to test whether or not someone else truly understands a sentence the way you intended is to ask that person (not the original author) to express the meaning of a requirement using different words. Ask them to rewrite it - **and not use any of your words**!

(Obvious exceptions are articles like "a", "an", "the", prepositions, and conjunctions, but it is critical that the other person is not allowed to use any of your nouns, verbs, adverbs or adjectives - the "meat" of the sentence.)

This little exercise actually forces the other person to think outside the box. It forces him or her to use terms that are different but mean the same thing to them. Once they finish, if you can read their sentence and it means the same to you as your original sentence, you can feel a lot more confident that you are getting your point across. If, however, you have to ask them why they used a specific word that you think means something different than you intended, that should be a red flag. You should probably consider revising your requirement to make sure that the two of you agree on a common meaning.

Look at a real-life example. The statement,

"The team of telephone operators should be able to complete up to 100 reservations per hour during peak volume"

---

looks like a reasonable requirement statement.

I gave this to a colleague and asked her to rewrite it following our rules. Her rewrite:

"The group of reservationists ought to be capable of finishing more than 99 requests for travel arrangements within a 60-minute period during the busiest times of the year."

Note first off that she changed "team of telephone operators" to "group of reservationists". Since those two phrases meant the same to both of us in the context of the project, there was no problem.

She also changed "should be able to complete" into "ought to be capable of finishing". I did not see any revelation in that change, so we were in accord.

She modified my "up to 100 reservations per hour" to read "more than 99 requests for travel arrangements within a 60-minute period".

Wow, that is actually quite different from what I meant. First off, "up to 100" sounds like an upper limit whereas "more than 99" sounds like a minimum. I had to clarify which the customer actually wanted before proceeding.

What about the difference between "per hour" and "within a 60-

minute period"? I could construe "per hour" to mean strictly by the clock, as in "from 8:00 am – 8:59 am" but 60 minutes could start and end anytime (which was what the subject matter expert really meant).

Exchanging "peak volume" for "the busiest times of the year" made sense, too, but that begged the question, "What was meant with 'times of the year'?" which got me thinking about the length of seasons and forced me to go back to my SME to get further clarification.

The team of telephone operators should be able to complete up to 100 reservations per hour during peak volume.

The group of reservationists ought to be capable of finishing more than 99 requests for travel arrangements within a 60 minute period during the busiest times of the year.

Picking the Right Peers

The name of this technique is "Peer Perception". You can see from the example that the simple act of analyzing the way someone else interpreted my original sentence was very revealing indeed. It gave me an insight into their thinking and could have potentially averted a costly miscommunication farther down the line. If you are going to try this little technique, two words of advice.

⇨ First off, since different genders often think differently, it might be a good idea to pick someone from the opposite sex to interpret your sentence.

⇨ Secondly, since different job functions require different thinking styles, you might ask a developer or designer (someone who will later actually have to understand the sentence) to do the rewrite.

Following these two recommendations should drastically improve the quality of your rewrites and the entire process of rewriting a requirement will definitely improve the quality of the delivered solution. As usual, here is an exercise to test your understanding of this concept.

Exercise: Requirement Interpretations

All exercises in this book are optional. They are online exercises that take anywhere from a few minutes to 20 minutes.

This is actually a two-part exercise. It will help you identify good requirement rewrites and then create your own rewrites.

In part one, you will see a requirement followed by five statements with checkboxes. Some of the statements are actual rewrites of the original requirement while others are not. Simply check all statements that you feel are legitimate rewrites and click the submit button. The program will offer feedback and insights that the rewrite provoked in the original author of the requirement. Take your time to be confident about your answer before you hit the submit button. In part two, we give you an opportunity to create your own rewrite.

To start the exercise, please go to http://goo.gl/ko5EUK

Now that you have tested your ability to recognize the rewritten requirements and had an opportunity to see some of the value provided by this technique, it is time for you to do your own rewrite. This time, you will see a requirement and a textbox in which you can enter your rewritten version. Remember the rules, you are not allowed to use any of the words in the original requirement except for articles (a, an, the), conjunctions (and, but, or), or prepositions (in, upon, without). As always, we will provide you our feedback once you have submitted your answer.

Press "Submit" to see the correct answers and our feedback.

To start the exercise, please go to http://goo.gl/romA1a

(DISCLAIMER: If you attempt the exercises on a standard PC, please use IE10 or higher or Chrome. They may not work on FireFox.)

Combatting the Major Cause of Project Failure

The overwhelming majority of research on IT project problems indicates that misunderstanding the meaning of requirements is a major cause for project overruns and failures.

The forced revision technique you just tried will help you identify where misinterpretation is possible. To reduce the potential for misunderstandings, you need to use words and phrases that can only be interpreted a certain way. For starters, the meaning of each word in a requirement has to be clear without referring to another requirement.

> 1. The system should add the sales tax to the total amount.
>
> ~~THE SALES TAX~~
> 2. It is 7% of the total amount.

Some words are inherently vague (like stuff and things) whereas others (such as the pronouns "it" or "them") can be easily misinterpreted.

An understandable business requirement has a single possible interpretation, meaning it

- ☑ leaves no doubt about the meaning of any of the words
- ☑ cannot be interpreted differently by different stakeholders

Consider the example,

"Applications should be processed by underwriters within 3 business days or they will be returned."

To what does the word "they" refer, the applications or the underwriters? Furthermore, the word "application" could be misinterpreted, meaning it is ambiguous. "Application" could refer to a computer application, a job application, or an application for insurance coverage.

To remove the ambiguity, change the word "applications" to "Insurance applications". You could argue that even that is ambiguous, since it could mean homeowners insurance, life insurance, or any other of the myriad types of insurance that the insurance industry tries to convince us that we cannot live without. Since our company only deals with automobile insurance, "Insurance applications" was clear enough within the context of the project. Putting the requirement in context is the simplest way of reducing ambiguity.

Next, we have the term, "should be processed". Even within the automobile insurance branch, there is a significant difference between processing claims, processing data, and processing applications so we definitely needed to clarify the term "processed". The term "approved or rejected" was what the SME really meant in this case. Of course, you cannot change the requirement by your authority as the business analyst / requirements engineer. Obviously, these clarifications involve the author / owner of the requirement (i.e., the appropriate SME).

Cool, now your revised business requirement reads

"Insurance applications which are not approved or rejected within 3 business days should be returned."

People are less likely to misinterpret that formulation of the requirement than the original. However, there is still the phrase in our rule that reads, "Cannot be interpreted differently by different stakeholders".

Our second example reads.

"Extensions should not be processed for accounts that are overdue."

In that requirement, "accounts that are overdue" could have had a very different meaning for accounting than for salespeople. Your job as the person-responsible-for-clarifying-this-requirement-is to try your best to discover the potential for misunderstanding and, as much as possible, stamp it out.

For instance, you could modify this requirement (based on interviews with the SME) to read:

"Policy extension requests from customers who owe us premium on their current policy should be rejected."

Revising, Defining, and Clarifying

Now that you know how to find ambiguity, the key question becomes what you can do about it. To show you, go back to our friend in the inventory manager role and we will try to figure out what to do about his requirement,

---

"The system should predict the amount of stuff we will sell."

Here are three specific activities that you can do to improve the understandability of this statement:

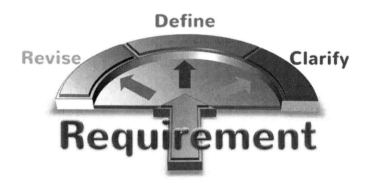

1. Revise it:

The system should predict the amount of **products** we will sell.

Replace obviously vague terms with a specific word that captures your meaning. For instance, replace the word "stuff" with "products". Vague terms are terms like "things", "stuff", "it". These words are blatantly ambiguous and can mean whatever the reader decides they should mean to make sense to the reader.

2. Define it:

The system should predict the **case lot quantities** of product that we will sell.

The next thing to look for are terms that are either too general in nature or could have multiple meanings. In our example, the word "amount" can have multiple meanings. You could replace the word "amount" with "case lot quantities". That might be too awkward (especially if the definition is too long), so you might leave the sentence unchanged but create a definition in a glossary where the reader can go to and get clarification. (**amount: quantity in case lot**)

3. Clarify it:

The system should predict the amount of products we will sell **during the next week**.

Finally, the requirement might be missing key information. If the requirement begs a question (i.e., "How far in the future do we have to predict sales?"), never leave the reader in suspense. Many people are afraid of asking questions for fear of appearing ignorant. (Actually, questions show interest, not ignorance, but that is a different story).

Instead of asking the obvious, they may "assume" that there is only one possible meaning and then develop a solution based on that assumption. Only when they deliver the solution will you see what they understood under your requirement. Add the missing information up front and avoid incorrect assumptions down the road. In our example, "during the next week" clarifies the statement by addressing the time dimension.

Exercise: Revising Requirements to Reduce Ambiguity

All exercises in this book are optional. They are online exercises that take anywhere from a few minutes to 20 minutes.

Deciding whether to expand an acronym, use a glossary, or replace a term with an industry standard could require some thought.

Having used the Peer Perception technique to ferret out potential misunderstandings, you need to use that newfound knowledge. We have another online exercise to show you words which we identified as ambiguous and you get to select a better term or phrase.

When you are done with the exercise, we will present other options for improving the understandability of a requirement.

To start the exercise, please go to http://goo.gl/LXVFYH

(DISCLAIMER: If you attempt the exercises on a standard PC, please use IE10 or higher or Chrome. They may not work on FireFox.)

Online resources for you:

Are you working in an Agile Environment?
Watch the following FREE videos:

⇨ How to Avoid Ambiguity in User Stories
  https://www.youtube.com/watch?v=BOIJGcDLZnE

⇨ Business Analysis and Agile Methodologies
  https://www.youtube.com/watch?v=z0LRrcIDog0

More online resources:

⇨ Writing Good Requirements: Ambiguous Terms to Avoid
  http://www.jamasoftware.com/wp-content/uploads/documents/Wiegers_Words_to_Avoid_Requirements.pdf

⇨ Ambiguity Reviews: Building Quality Requirements
  http://www.slideshare.net/TechWellPresentations/ambiguity-reviews-building-quality-requirements

⇨ Mind the Gap: Addressing Ambiguity in Requirements
  http://blog.lansa.com/application-development/ambiguity-in-requirements

⇨ 7 Steps to Avoid the Ambiguous Requirement and Maybe See a Unicorn
  https://www.netcentric.biz/blog/2015/05/avoid-ambiguous-requirement.html

⇨ FREE Business Analysis Videos
  http://businessanalysisexperts.com/product-category/free-business-analysis-training/

BEST PRACTICES FOR
IMPROVING UNDERSTANDABILITY

This chapter will help you:

- ⇨ Make Appropriate Use of Acronyms
- ⇨ Use Corporate and Industry Standards
- ⇨ Understand the Power of a Glossary
- ⇨ Add Context and Other Missing Information

Because ambiguity is such a major problem in requirements, we would like to continue our quest to reduce it as much as possible before we pass the requirements on to the solution providers.

In this chapter, we introduce three specific techniques which combined will significantly reduce the likelihood of other stakeholders (e.g., Subject Matter Experts and solution providers) misinterpreting your requirements.

This chapter also contains a recap of the ambiguity rule (Rule 4) and your "Final Exam" in applying these powerful techniques to improve the understandability of your requirements.

Use Acronyms and Corporate Standards

People have a better chance at understanding a requirement if it:

⇨ defines or expands all acronyms for clarity

⇨ includes corporate or industry standard terms wherever possible

⇨ uses glossary entries that are obvious to the reader

Acronyms, Yes, BUT …

Take a good, hard look at any acronym you are using. Acronyms are a phenomenally effective tool for communication – if you use them correctly. They are also one of the best methods for confusion if you do not. If the acronym is a corporate or industry standard term, you might get by without expanding it, but I would recommend against even that.

You can certainly use acronyms in your requirements statements (why write 'Federal Emergency Management Agency' every time you refer to FEMA). The biggest risk in using acronyms is that they come in bunches, so make sure that you attach a list of the acronyms you are using with their specific expansions. Your target audience really needs to know what you are referring to when they read FEMA.

What could FEMA possibly be? The examples above are just a smattering of potential expansions of the FEMA acronym. By the way, never use the same acronym to mean two different things in a single document. That is a certain recipe for miscommunication.

Make Use of Corporate and Industry Standards

Another simple idea for improving communication is to use corporate or industry standard terms. If there is somewhere that anyone can go to get a common definition of a term, you can legitimately claim that the meaning of that term is clear within the context of your organization or industry.

For instance, the words "policy" and "premium" have a very distinct meaning in the insurance industry. The key question then becomes how to recognize terms and phrases that you should replace with a corporate standard.

In interviewing or just chatting with your SME's, listen for words that they feel compelled to explain. Alternatively, if you feel that you need to ask about how they mean a specific term, ask whether it is a common term in their field. If it is, ask where you can get an "official" definition of the term.

In addition, if your organization has a Standards Committee you might check with them about the availability of a "corporate dictionary". Of course, it is a nice gesture if you let your target audience know somehow where they need to go to get those definitions.

The Power of a Glossary

If you do not have industry or corporate standard definitions, use standard terms or words that a glossary of terms clearly defines. If you do not have a glossary yet, now is a great time to start building one. Over time, it will help you a lot in making communication amongst your peers easier and more effective.

To make effective use of current technology, consider hyper-linking defined terms directly to their definition in the glossary, either each time it is used or at least the first use within the document. Always try to make it as easy as possible on anyone who has to understand or work with your requirements.

If you cannot hyper-link them, then make sure the reader knows that you have a glossary entry for this term. You might want to make it bold, italic or a different color but, if you do, stay consistent and use that formatting feature only for words that you define in the glossary.

If you design your document to be readable in a browser, you might even consider using rollover technology to define the term. A simple exercise might clarify this process.

Exercise: Using Revisions to Reduce Ambiguity

All exercises in this book are optional. They are online exercises that take anywhere from a few minutes to 20 minutes.

Deciding whether to expand an acronym, use a glossary, or replace a term with an industry standard could require some thought. In this exercise, we will present a set of potential actions that might improve the understandability of the highlighted term. Choose the best alternative and click on the "Submit" button to see our recommended actions and rationale.

To start the exercise, please go to http://goo.gl/I4Q0Qh

(DISCLAIMER: If you attempt the exercises on a standard PC, please use IE10 or higher or Chrome. They may not work on FireFox.)

Add Context to Eliminate Ambiguity

An unambiguous business requirement avoids confusion by

⇨ adding context to clarify any term or phrase that needs it

⇨ adding any other missing information needed for clarity

Ambiguity refers to a word, a phrase, a sentence, or even an entire paragraph that has potentially different meanings to different people. The only way to remove ambiguity is by adding context to any word or phrase that needs it OR adding other, missing information needed for clarity.

Look at the two sentences presented here:

---

1. "Raymond watched the bat flitting through the air."

2. "Raymond gripped the bat tightly."

What comes to your mind reading these two sentences? Does the word "bat" refer to a piece of sport equipment for striking a baseball or a nocturnal animal associated with vampires? Did you think of either possibility or just one?

An unambiguous statement has only one possible meaning to the target audience. Ambiguous requirements might be missing contextual information meaning information that would make the requirement understandable.

If the requirement begs a question (for example, "What kind of a bat?"), do not leave the reader in suspense.

"Raymond gripped the **baseball** bat tightly"

adds context while

"Raymond watched the bat flitting through the air **using its sonar to guide it**"

added clarifying information.

You may remember the requirement from a previous example:

"Insurance applications which are not approved or rejected within 3 business days will be returned."

You modified an earlier version to remove vague terms, but there is still some ambiguity remaining.

For example, when do "3 business days" start and when do they end? Assume you receive the application at 1 minute before midnight Friday. Does it have to be processed by midnight Tuesday (1 minute of the first business day and 2 full business days), or by midnight Wednesday (1 minute of the first business day and 3 full business days)?

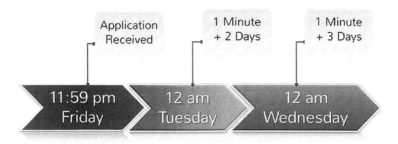

After digging deeper, you discover that neither of them is right because "3 business days" means "by the close of business on the 3rd business day after receipt".

Now your revised business requirement reads,

"Insurance applications which are not approved or rejected by the close of business on the 3rd business day after receipt will be returned."

That is unambiguous within the context of our project. Of course, you could get into time zones and geographic locations of the applicant versus the processor (and you would have to if it mattered), but since you do not have to, I will leave that as a mental exercise for you to resolve.

Another example is the statement,

"Telephone operators should process 100 calls per hour."

Does the term "Telephone operators" refer to each individual operator or to the group of operators as a whole? As before, what does the term "process" mean in this context? Even the simple phrase "per hour" needs clarification, does that mean during any hour or any day of any month? Once you get the subject matter expert to rephrase the statement as,

"The team of telephone operators taking reservations should be able to complete up to 100 reservations per hour during peak volume."

the sentence – and the intent behind it - starts to become clearer.

Having presented this concept, I think that it is time for an exercise!

Exercise: Appropriate Context Reduces Ambiguity

All exercises in this book are optional. They are online exercises that take anywhere from a few minutes to 20 minutes.

Deciding whether to expand an acronym, use a glossary, or replace a term with an industry standard could require some thought.

In this exercise, we will present a set of potential actions that might improve the understandability of the highlighted term. Choose the best alternative and click on the "Submit" button to see our recommended actions and rationale.

To start the exercise, please go to http://goo.gl/5txDfJ

(DISCLAIMER: If you attempt the exercises on a standard PC, please use IE10 or higher or Chrome. They may not work on FireFox.)

Write to the Readability Level of Your Audience

An easily understandable requirement is written to the readability level of the target audience by

staying within standard readability indices (6th grade?).

To improve the understandability of your requirements, we recommend that you know what **standard readability indices** are and use them. (In the event that you are unfamiliar with the concept, we recommend http://en.wikipedia.org/wiki/Readability_test).

Some organizations have readability standards for documentation that leaves the organization or that focuses on a specific audience. Unfortunately, not many use this phenomenally simple concept in their internal communication and even less use it for requirements definition documents.

Most word processors offer you the ability to check the grade level readability index of a document. For instance, if you are using Microsoft Word®, the option is available in the "Spelling and Grammar" although you have to turn it on in your "Options". You can also use the free website "readability-score.com".

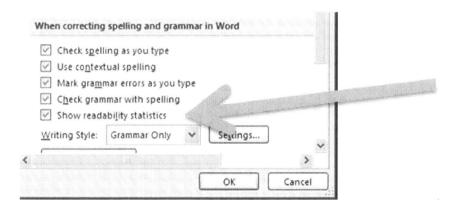

Measuring Readability

To give you the flavor of readability levels, consider the requirement statement,

---

"The system should extrapolate the point of origination, point of termination, and the duration adjusted for inclusive time zones as enabling factors of the connection cost calculation algorithm."

This little gem comes in at **grade level 18.5**, which means only 12% of the general population can easily understand it.

Change it to read,

"The system should determine the calling party, the called party, and the duration adjusted for time zones to calculate the connection cost."

Now it measures **grade level 12.2** or, in other words, about 46% of the English-speaking population as a whole can now understand it.

You can further simplify the requirement by splitting it into two statements.

---

1. "The system should use the area code the call comes from and the area code being called to compute the cost of a call."

2. "The length of the call must take time zones into account."

This combination now scores grade level 5.0, so nearly 90% of the general population can be expected to understand it. Which one would you rather work with?

As a general rule 8th grade level makes it easier on your target audience. In addition, consider that your target audience might be foreigners who may have an excellent education – and might even speak English better than we do – but they might miss the meanings of idioms and contractions, so avoid them as much as possible.

A DROP IN THE BUCKET
A PIECE OF CAKE
A TOSS-UP
AT THE DROP OF A HAT

We realize that the abstract concept of readability indices is not one that you can readily apply while you are writing a requirement. We do, however, know from experience that you can improve the understandability of a set of business requirements by using this simple tool to get a better idea of what level they are written for and, possibly, revising them to make them simpler.

Exercise: Using Readability Indices

All exercises in this book are optional. They are online exercises that take anywhere from a few minutes to 20 minutes.

What readability level do you score?

In this exercise, read each requirement and guess at its grade level. Check your answer by clicking the "Submit" button. If you prefer, put it into your favorite word processor (or the web app) and run the spell checker to get the official readability index.

To start the exercise, please go to http://goo.gl/QxGZbo

(DISCLAIMER: If you attempt the exercises on a standard PC, please use IE10 or higher or Chrome. They may not work on FireFox.)

Recap Rule Four

An effective Requirement Statement is understandable, unambiguous, and clear to the target audience, meaning it:

⇨ Cannot be interpreted differently by different stakeholders because it has a single possible interpretation that leaves no doubt about the meaning of any of the words

⇨ Is easily understood by knowledge peers by expanding all acronyms, using corporate or industry standard terms wherever possible, and defining critical terms in an understandable glossary

⇨ Avoids confusion by staying in context and adding supplementary information to any term or phrase that can be misinterpreted within the context

⇨ Is appropriate for all target audiences by using standard readability indices

Given all that new knowledge it is time to put it all together into a final test of your understanding of this philosophy.

Exercise: Rule Four Applied

All exercises in this book are optional. They are online exercises that take anywhere from a few minutes to 20 minutes.

A Reality Check of Ambiguity

This is the last exercise in this book, so you are almost there! We are going to present you with background information from again a different project along with several requirements. Your assignment is to determine whether each requirement complies with each part of rule 4. As a recommended approach, check each requirement one part at a time and if it violates any part of the rule, move on to the next requirement. Check the box only if the requirement meets all parts of the rule.

To start the exercise, please go to http://goo.gl/Ut48zm

(DISCLAIMER: If you attempt the exercises on a standard PC, please use IE10 or higher or Chrome. They may not work on FireFox.)

Online resources for you:

⇨ The Quest For Good Requirements
   https://www.batimes.com/articles/the-quest-for-good-requirements.html

⇨ Karl Wiegers Describes 10 Requirements Traps to Avoid
   http://processimpact.com/articles/reqtraps.html

⇨ Managing ambiguity – a key business analyst competency
   http://www.bridging-the-gap.com/managing-ambiguity-a-key-business-analyst-competency/

⇨ Avoiding Ambiguity in Requirements Specifications
   https://cs.uwaterloo.ca/~dberry/FTP_SITE/students.theses/TjongThesis.pdf

⇨ Taming Ambiguity in Natural Language Requirements
   http://citeseerx.ist.psu.edu/viewdoc/download?doi=10.1.1.456.1925&rep=rep1&type=pdf

⇨ Characteristics of a Good Requirement
   http://www.informit.com/articles/article.aspx?p=1152528&seqNum=4

⇨ Ambiguity in Stating Requirements
   http://www.dorsethouse.com/features/excerpts/exerch2.html

⇨ Your Personalized Business Analysis Skills Evaluation
   http://businessanalysisexperts.com/BASE/business-analyst-skills-self-assessment.html

⇨ FREE Business Analysis Videos
   http://businessanalysisexperts.com/product-category/free-business-analysis-training/

WHERE DOES YOUR PATH GO FROM HERE?

Thank you for buying, "Writing Requirements for IT — Simply Put!". We trust that you enjoyed the book, hope that you are able to integrate the presented ideas into your life, and that they serve you well when you are the one wearing the business analysis hat.

Any feedback you provide helps us improve the learning experience for all students. Please leave a review on Amazon or our website to capture your feedback. If you have any issues to report, we will respond as quickly as possible.

This book is just one component of our blended learning curriculum. Our discovery learning-based training approach and our other delivery methods (onsite/online classroom, self-paced eCourses, eBooks, and eMentoring) augment books such as this and allow you to select the appropriate combination to build your business analysis skills while containing costs. Check our Business Analysis Training Store (http://businessanalysisexperts.com/business-analysis-training-store/) for a complete overview of all of our training offers for the one wearing the BA hat.

Meanwhile, thank you again for buying this book. Use your new-found business analysis knowledge to achieve your personal and professional goals.

ABOUT THE AUTHORS

Angela and Tom Hathaway have authored and delivered hundreds of training courses and publications for business analysts around the world. They have facilitated hundreds of requirements discovery sessions for information technology projects under a variety of acronyms (JAD, ASAP, JADr, JRP, etc.). Based on their personal journey and experiences reported by their students, they recognized how much anyone can benefit from improving their requirements elicitation skills.

Angela's and Tom's mission is to allow anyone, anywhere access to simple, easy-to-learn business analysis techniques by sharing their experience and expertise in their business analysis training seminars, blogs, books, and public presentations.

At BA-EXPERTS (http://businessanalysisexperts.com/) we focus exclusively on Business Analysis for **"anyone wearing the BA hat™"**. We believe that business analysis has become a needed skill for every business professional whether or not they have the title Business Analyst. We have made it our goal to enable anyone wearing the BA hat™ to have access to high quality training material and performance support. Please call us at 702-637-4573, email us (Tom.Hathaway@ba-experts.com), or visit our Business Analyst Learning Store at (http://businessanalysisexperts.com/business-analysis-training-store/) if you are interested in other training offers. Amongst other offers, the content of this book is also available as an eCourse on our website.

Made in the USA
Monee, IL
12 November 2019